Andrea Scholtz

Design Classics

le 1020
ente

Verlag form

Just who was Johannes Potente? Quite a few people may have asked themselves that very question when the door handle company Franz Schneider Brakel, FSB for short, prepared a book titled *Johannes Potente, Brakel – Design der 50er Jahre* [1] for 1988. Nobody had ever heard of him. The door handles had no name – they could only be identified by number. And then, suddenly, there was a designer for them. And, on top of everything, there was this last name sounding so unusual and so Italian, for Westphalian conditions at any rate, following the very German first name. It all sounded like a clever advertising gag, the brainchild of a smart marketing director.

But Johannes Potente really did exist. Otl Aicher, who developed the corporate identity for FSB, had discovered him. Aicher also had the idea to make a book about the thus far unknown designer. About his meeting with Potente he wrote: "if you suddenly come across a designer like Johannes Potente, and you enjoy him and his work, and you find his traces everywhere, both good and bad, and you see how he left his mark especially on the fifties, then it doesn't seem right to remove him from his position of historical anonymity and integrate him into the history of design; he shall stay who he was, an anonymous designer." [2]

During the exploration and reconstruction of their own history, FSB realized the importance of Johannes Potente's work. Otl Aicher together with Jürgen W. Braun, the manager of the enterprise, visited the pensioner at his home. Aicher, for whom "design is anonymous in its substance", thought of Potente as somebody who designs something because it is needed, not because he wants to become famous: "...Johannes Potente was surprised at the notion of being a designer. He was a layman. He made models for door handles simply because there was a need for them and because he had the talent to carry out the task." This is how Otl Aicher characterized the unknown form designer. [3]

The preceding page shows Johannes Potente during the fifties at his first drawing board, which he purchased himself and brought into the enterprise. In front: half of a mould.

Furniture fittings, here in the 1927 catalog, were one of the major fields of production for FSB until the early fifties. Johannes Potente, an apprenticed steel engraver, made tools and forms for them.

A life for door handles

Johannes Potente wasn't trained as a designer. He was a professional steel engraver, and that is how he wanted to be addressed.

Steel engravers were highly sought after back then. They produced the tools and forms for the production of fixtures – for example, for furniture, FSB's most important field of production up to the fifties. They had to possess the skills of the draftsman and they needed excellent manual

skills. "They were almost artists; they stood out against the others simply in their appearance. During work they wore white coats with a collar and tie." [4]

In stark contrast to the present – this work is now done by machines – the forms and tools were manually worked from the steel cubes with a hammer and chisel. The engravers did the filigree work with gouges, punches and so-called riffle irons. The fixtures were then cast from the negative forms. Especially precious pieces were finished by the engravers through chasing.

In all his life, Johannes Potente hardly ever moved from his hometown of Brakel in the Weserbergland in eastern Westphalia. He was born there on 9 September 1908, and he died there on 11 May 1987. In between there were only a few milestones in his life. After he had finished school in 1922 at age 14, he began an apprenticeship as a steel engraver with the Westphalian Metal Works Franz Schneider in Brakel, as FSB was called back in those days. It was a much smaller enterprise back then, with fewer than 100 employees. But, as is still true today, it was the largest employer in town. In 1926, Johannes Potente finished his training. [5] Afterwards, he was employed by the Westphalian Metal Works. He was known as an "engraver's assistant, working cleanly and quickly". [6] Before World War II Franz Schneider had already begun to realize that "aside from the quality, the beautiful form of the products appropriate to the nature of the material would be a principle condition for marketability and sales". [7] Therefore, he chose Johannes Potente as a technical form designer and provided him with additional training. Starting with the

Steel engravers were sought-after and respected people. They distinguished themselves in their manner of dress, with a tie and white work coats, from the others. In front are the masters, with Johannes Potente in the center, and in the back are the journeymen and one apprentice.

winter semester 1932/33, Potente spent two terms at the Badische Kunstgewerbeschule (school of Arts and Crafts) in Pforzheim where he took classes on subjects like modeling, free-hand drawing, geometric drawing, type, style theory, engraving and chasing. It's possible that he visited a master course, but it remains unclear why he left school before finishing his studies – it's something he never talked about. [8] A short time thereafter, in 1934, Johannes Potente was given the job as head of the steel engraving department with Franz Schneider. Four years later, on 1 September 1938, he became the master of the steel engraving, tool-making and industrial training departments. That same month he married Therese Groppe from Brakel; they would have five sons.

In 1951, the first catalog following the war shows the door handles that were again being produced: the old pre-war models made of bakelite and sheet metal, so-called nickel horn handles.

During World War II he was sent to the eastern front from 1940 to 1945. He was with the military engineers and drew mine laying maps. After his return from war prison working at a vineyard in France, Potente went back to work with the Westphalian Metal Works in Brakel. In 1950 he became the head of development, design, tool-making, engraving and industrial training departments.

During the fifties, Potente designed his first door handles. FSB no longer wanted to simply produce the old pre-war models but their own newly-designed handles. On the side, Johannes Potente designed what was needed, and he clearly put his own personal mark on the product palette especially during that period of time with FSB. In the 1957 anniversary publication – though without his name being mentioned – he was already being referred to as "the form designer of the works" and was portrayed

TÜRBESCHLÄGE
echt nickelplattiert
FSB
handlich - stets sauber
unverwüstlich
rostsicher
und sehr preiswert

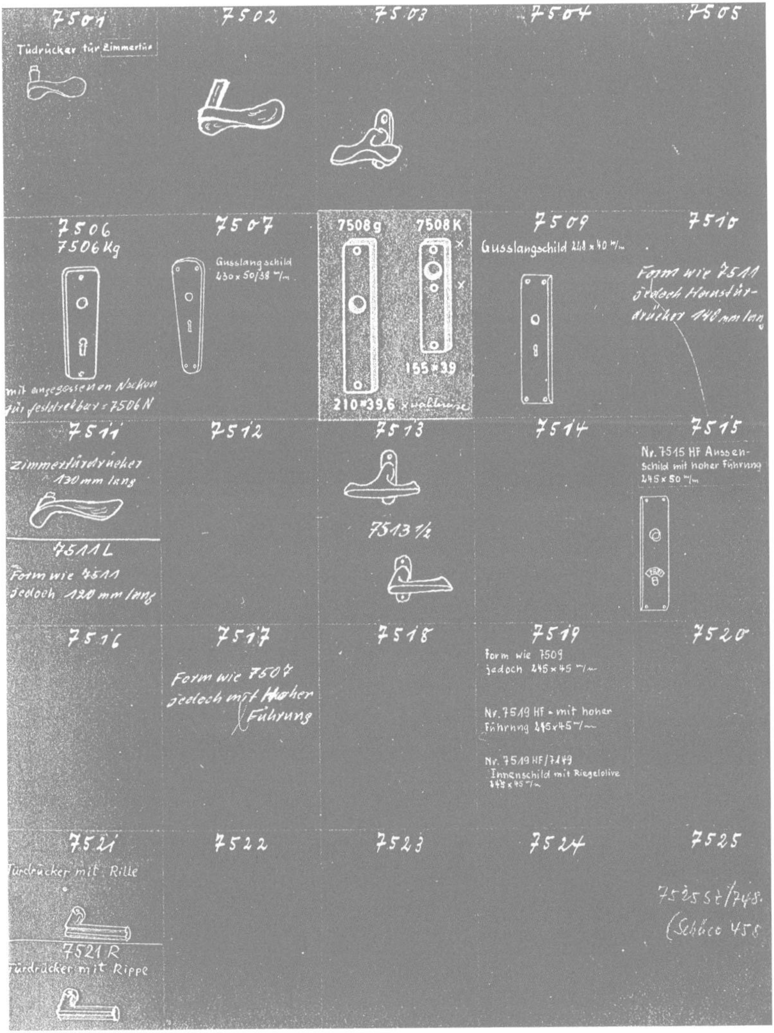
7501
Türdrücker für Zimmertür
7502
7503
7504
7505
7506
7506 Kg
mit angegossenen Nocken für feststellbar = 7506 N
7507
Gusslangschild 430 x 50/38 m/m
7508 g
7508 K
155 x 39
210 x 39,6
7509
Gusslangschild 248 x 40 m/m
7510
Form wie 7511 jedoch Haustürdrücker 148 mm lang
7511
Zimmertürdrücker 130 mm lang
7511 L
Form wie 7511 jedoch 120 mm lang
7512
7513
7513 1/2
7514
7515
Nr. 7515 HF Aussen-schild mit hoher Führung 245 x 50 m/m
7516
7517
Form wie 7507 jedoch mit hoher Führung
7518
7519
Form wie 7509 jedoch 245 x 45 m/m
Nr. 7519 HF = mit hoher Führung 245 x 45 m/m
Nr. 7519 HF/7149 Innenschild mit Riegelolive 245 x 45 m/m
7520
7521
Türdrücker mit Rille
7521 R
Türdrücker mit Rippe
7522
7523
7524
7525
7525 St/748.
(Schüco 458

in a picture with drawing board and file and brought into context with Raymond Loewy's views on industrial design. Even after retiring in 1973, he didn't stop designing door handles. Jürgen W. Braun, manager with FSB since 1981, set up a small workshop for him and brought him back into the enterprise. Until shortly before his death, Johannes Potente worked in this workshop almost every day.

"To him there really was only the company. It was his entire life's oeuvre. He started at six in the morning and left at seven or eight at night. He knew nothing but work. Once he said that if he didn't smell the factory air, he'd become sick, that the factory air was his medicine", remembers Helmuth Beine, who was trained by Johannes Potente and who today is the head of the construction department at FSB. [9] What has stuck in the memories as well are the evenings of convivial drinking around the workbench at special occasions such as birthdays or similar events, where everybody sang upon Potente's command.

Otl Aicher characterized this form designer, who was as unspectacular as he was unpretentious, as follows: "Johannes Potente thought about door handles and not about art history. He stayed with the subject and with his work. Indeed, he behaved just as trivially as the object itself. But this doesn't mean that he didn't care about door handles. On the contrary, he lived for them, but only in the context of their use, their production, and their fabrication – not in the context of their reputation." [10] The profession – the self-understanding of the designer as being also an intellectual "cultural worker" with a concurrent level of status – was foreign concept to Potente.

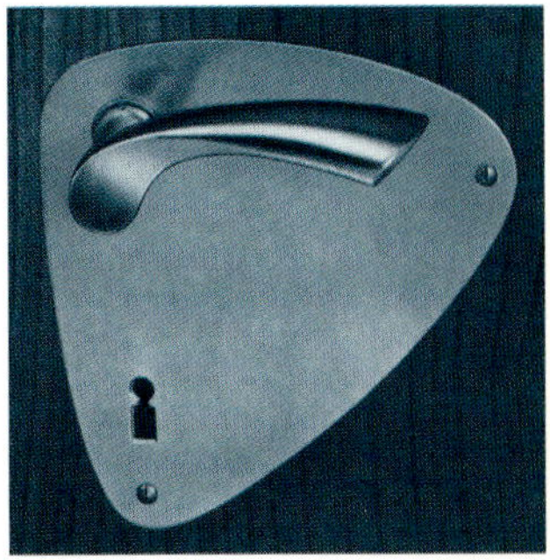

Model 1034 (formerly 7581) was offered in the 1957 catalog with a wide plate that was reminiscent of the kidney-shaped tables from the fifties.

In this sketchbook, the separate products were drawn and provided with a product number. On the top left: the model 1020, formerly number 7501.

This was enough reason for Otl Aicher to think of him as a true designer in the original sense – "a craftsman who designed".

Reconstruction, economic miracle, building boom

From 1957 onward there was a rosette for the door handle 1020 in addition to the long plates. It was decorated with an all-round, set-off ring.

FSB delivers fittings throughout the world. This is what one could read in 1957 in the 75th anniversary brochure.

After World War II, the stream of refugees from the east led to a dramatic housing shortage in the bombed-out German cities. In 1948 monetary reform was enacted, storefronts slowly began to fill again, reconstruction began. Consumers had a lot of catching up to do. The industrial enterprises at first resumed the production of pre-war products. By 1950, the production levels of the pre-war era had been achieved. There was a wave of consumerism, the economic upswing had arrived. Housing construction became one of the most important areas during the fifties. Between 1949 and 1960 the federal government, the states and communities built approximately five million apartments. [11] In 1954 alone, the year when Potente's door handle 1020 was launched onto the market, 542, 800 apartments were built. Thus, the Federal Republic had, by far, more apartments per 1000 inhabitants than any other European country. [12]

The building boom during the fifties also created an enormous upswing for the fixture industry. Like other enterprises, FSB could restart their production of building and furniture fixtures only after the monetary reform that went into effect on 20 June 1948. From the end of the war, in 1945, to 1948, the enterprise was at an almost complete standstill. By 1956, almost 400 employees worked there, more than twice as many as during the best times

N
W
O
S
FSB
in alle Welt!
Nr. 7509
F2
10 Paar
Nr. 7581
F2
5 Paar
Nr. 7529
F2
5 Paar

Sie läuft und läuft und läuft.

FSB

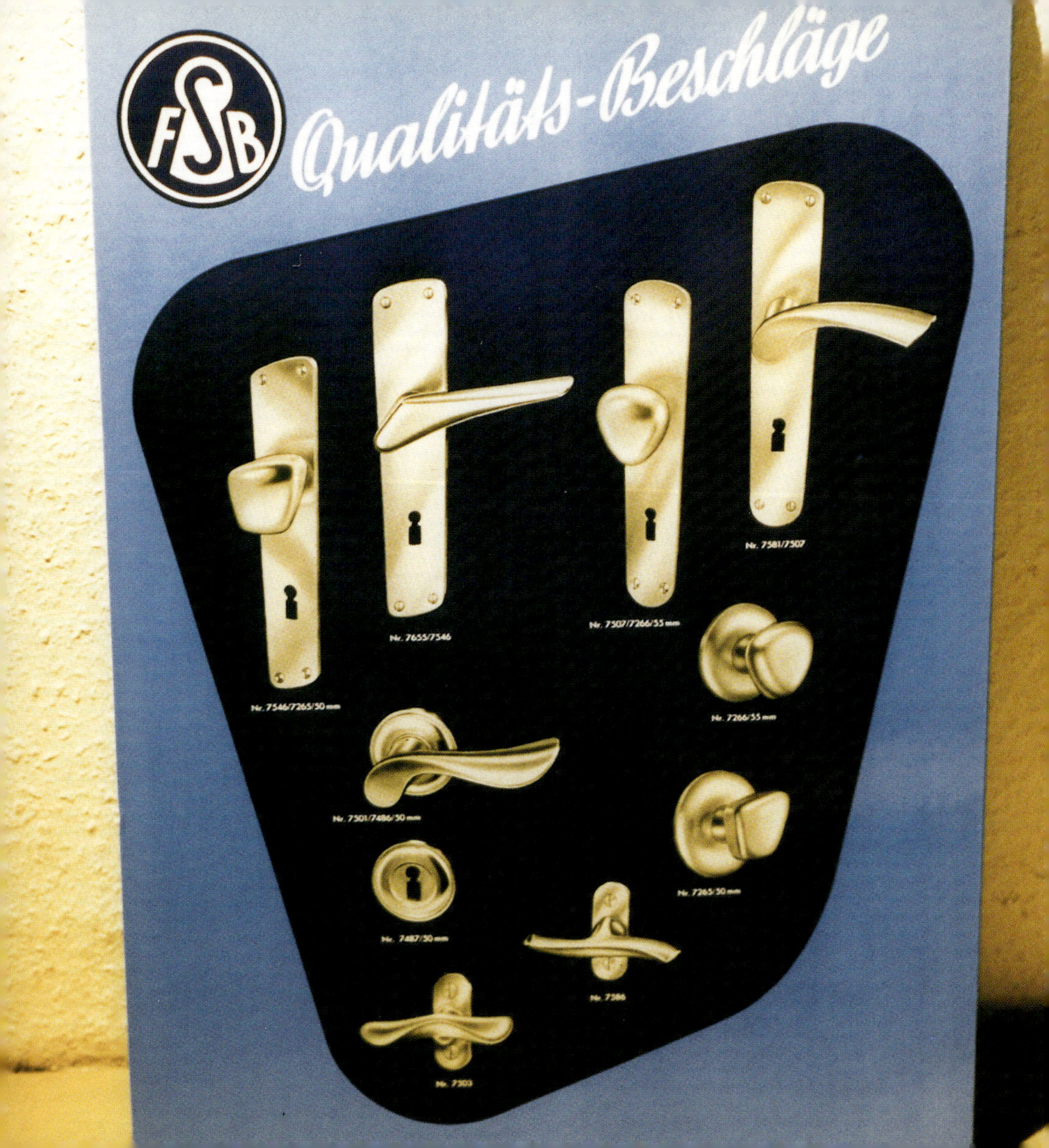
FSB
Qualitäts-Beschläge
Nr. 7581/7507
Nr. 7655/7546
Nr. 7507/7266/55 mm
Nr. 7546/7265/50 mm
Nr. 7266/55 mm
Nr. 7501/7486/50 mm
Nr. 7265/50 mm
Nr. 7487/50 mm
Nr. 7586
Nr. 7503

before the war (160 employees). In addition to their furniture fixtures, FSB had started producing light metal building fixtures in the late twenties, and the first door fixtures were produced in the thirties; however, these were generally very commonplace models: door handles made of Bakelite and sheet metal, the so-called nickel horn handles. During the fifties, production concentrated increasingly on building fixtures; the furniture fixtures were pushed into the background. It thus became necessary to design an assortment of building fixtures, and Johannes Potente was entrusted with this task. While the first catalog in 1951 still presented door handle models dating back to the pre-war era, the subsequent catalog in 1955 offered an assortment of new door handle models by Johannes Potente.

One of the first door handles Johannes Potente realized was the model 7581 (today 1034) designed in 1952. It came onto the market in 1953 and quickly became a success, which later led to the nickname "million handle". A 1993/94 advertising campaign compared the handle with the VW *Beetle* and adopted the motto "it runs and runs and runs".

In 1953 Johannes Potente developed the next door handle: the model 1020 (originally 7501). "Although 1034 was an absolute hit, 1020 attracted more attention through its design because it was such a typical product for that time", remembers Dieter Eller, a nephew and former apprentice of Potente and today's head of the product development department of FSB. [13]

The most striking feature of this door handle is its orga-

Preceding double page: the advertising campaign "It runs and runs and runs" juxtaposed the success of the "million handle" 1034 with that of the VW bug.

Billboard from the fifties with the first door handles by Johannes Potente: the *Brakel beak*, the "million handle" and model 1020. During the fifties, the rosette was still decorated with a ring; today (top) it has a clear and reduced form. Two different window handles are part of the 1020 product family: the window olive and semi-olive.

nic curve, which runs through the model like a long wave and forms a contrast with the lines and right angles of the doors. Like a beacon, it attracts looks. In the turning point, the kidney shape typical for the time is discernible. Seen from above, the handle widens almost unnoticeably at first and then strongly swells up towards the end of the handle. This is reminiscent of the back of a spoon. It's no coincidence that the handle was sometimes called "spoon handle" within the enterprise, or more poetically, "wing beat" or "butterfly". The molded-to-the-hand fixture, with its undulating curve, visually pretends a symmetry that really doesn't exist. From the front, the curve appears to be a horizontal S-curve.

The four laws of grasping: thumb stop, index finger hollow, ball support and grasping volume.

From 1958/59 onward, technical drawings were made at FSB. Here: a drawing of model 1020 by Helmuth Beine, a former apprentice.

With his model 1020, as is the case with most of his other handles, Johannes Potente had already intuitively realized the "four laws of grasping", which were formulated in 1986 by Otl Aicher in the book *Greifen und Griffe*:
1. the thumb seeks and finds its place on the thumb stop
2. the index finger finds its (index finger) hollow
3. the hand is supported by the ball support
4. no hand likes to reach into a void. Therefore, it needs its grasping volume.

The product family

Altogether, three handles were produced in the shape of the 1020. The first was an interior room door handle with a length of 13 centimeters, followed by a front door handle with a length of 14 centimeters (formerly no. 7500). A little later, probably in 1954, the model 7501 L (light) was added. Lighter weight doors were put on the market

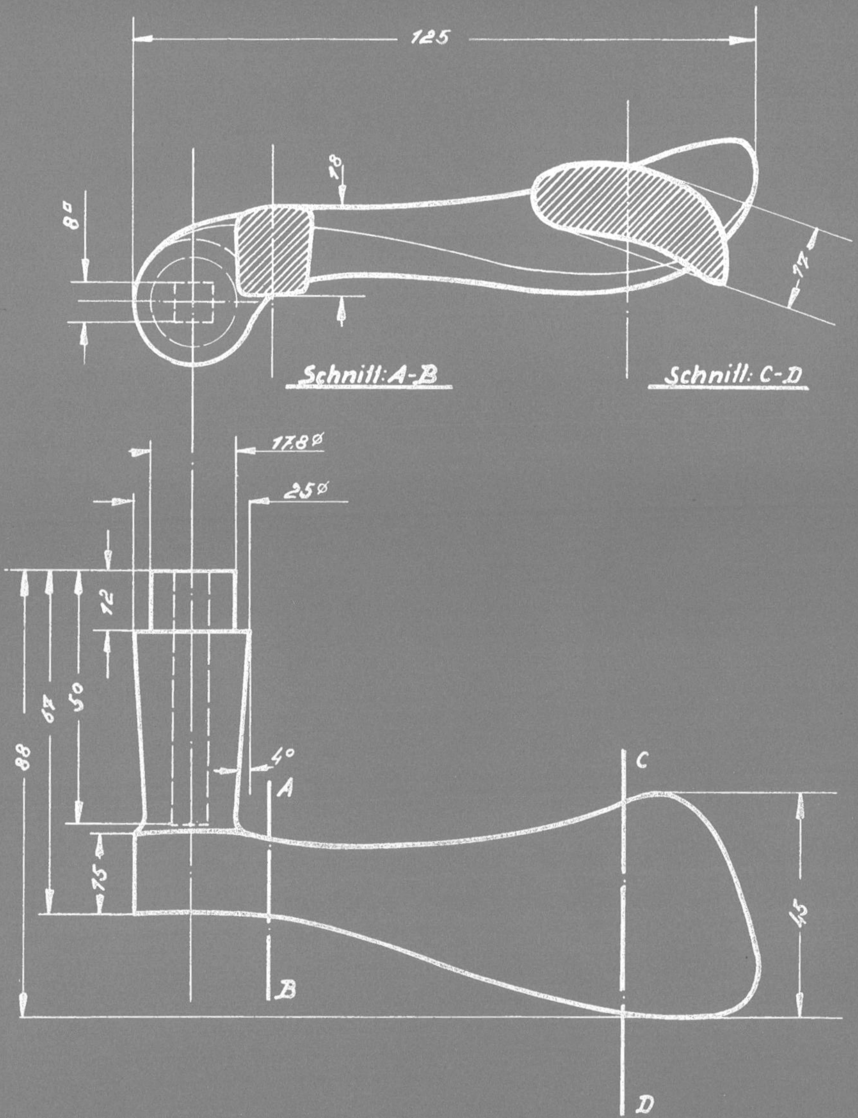
125
18
8
17
Schnitt: A-B
Schnitt: C-D
17,8 Ø
25 Ø
12
50
67
88
15
4°
A
B
C
D
45

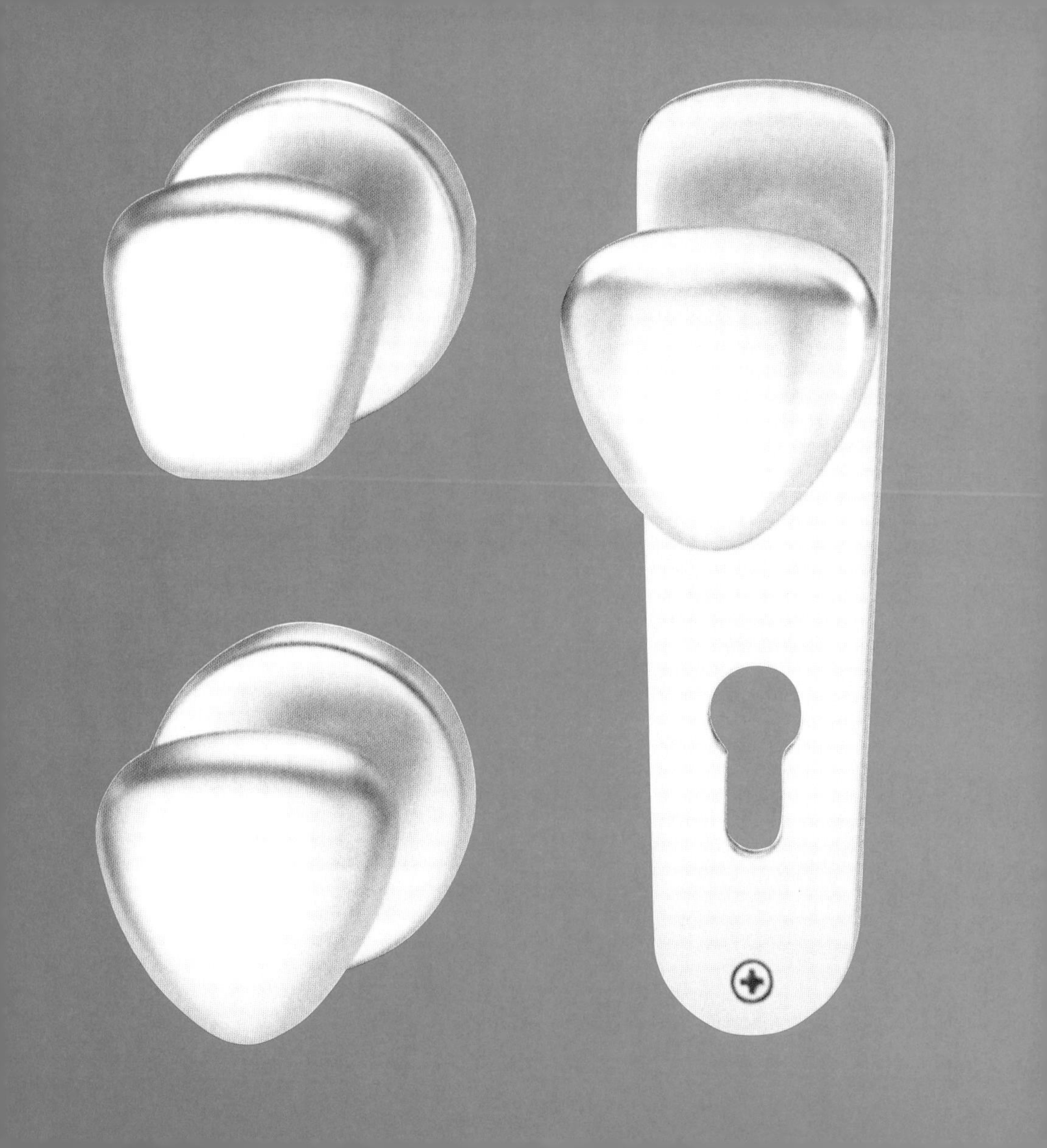

back then, and for them an appropriately smaller door handle was needed. Therefore, the smallest handle in the family was only 11,5 centimeters long. [14]

From the two sizes for room doors, a single model in a medium size emerged over the course of time. The shape was continuously changed and improved. Today, the handle is available in light metal (aluminum) in various colors and in brass.

For the exterior handles for front doors, Johannes Potente at first (c. 1954) designed a heart-shaped door knob (7266, today 0817) that took up the organically curved forms of the first two handle models (1034 and 1020). The "heart knob", with its new and unusual form, contrasted with the common door knobs in the shape of a sphere or discus. In 1956, Potente presented another knob, this time in the shape of a trapezoid, which can be more easily grabbed (today 0810). The clear and straight-lined handle designs of the following period rather follow this calmer, geometric form.

In the 1955 catalog, a long cover plate, which narrows towards the bottom and terminates in a semi-circle while the upper termination is formed by a light semi-arch and rounded edges, is offered for the door handles (7507). For the model 1020 Potente designed an asymmetrical and somewhat organically formed long cover plate that thoroughly expressed the spirit of the fifties (7547 and 7567). From 1957 onward, a rosette decorated with an all-round set-off ring was offered in addition to the long cover plate (7486). Its round shape conforms more with the soft organic form of the handle than does the long door

Johannes Potente designed two door handles for the outside of the entrance door: one with a heart shape (c. 1954), and one with a trapezoid shape. Their unusual forms set them apart from the spheroid and discus-shaped door handles of the time.

plate. The handle is offered with the rosette up to this day; however, now it is rather simple and has no ornamentation. Included in the model 1020 product family are also two window handles: a window olive handle with two symmetrical wings (3404), and a semi-olive handle that takes up the door handle shape but in a smaller format (3405). Both are still being produced today.

„We ought to be able to sell this..."

Numerous steps are necessary before an every-day-product like a door handle is finished. From the initial concept to the final product, Potente needed about half a year.

At first he had drawn a sketch[15] for the 1020 design, then he made a wooden model. Thereafter, the apprentices had to prepare the shape of the handle in aluminum. "You got an aluminum block about 15 centimeters long and three to four centimeters thick. Potente had roughly drawn the form onto it, the lines were partially perforated with a center punch. We had to saw and file out the contours," recalls Helmuth Beine, one of the apprentices during the fifties. Johannes Potente asked a lot from them. "If a block had been worked by us too long or too short, we had to redo it. A couple of harsh words were spoken and our ears pulled if things didn't quite work out." Once the work had met with his approval, Potente gave it the fine finish. Helmuth Beine described the discovery of a suitable door handle form as follows: "It often happened that such a model would be discarded four or five times. He would then hold the handle in his hand for days and would touch and feel it." Most of the time he

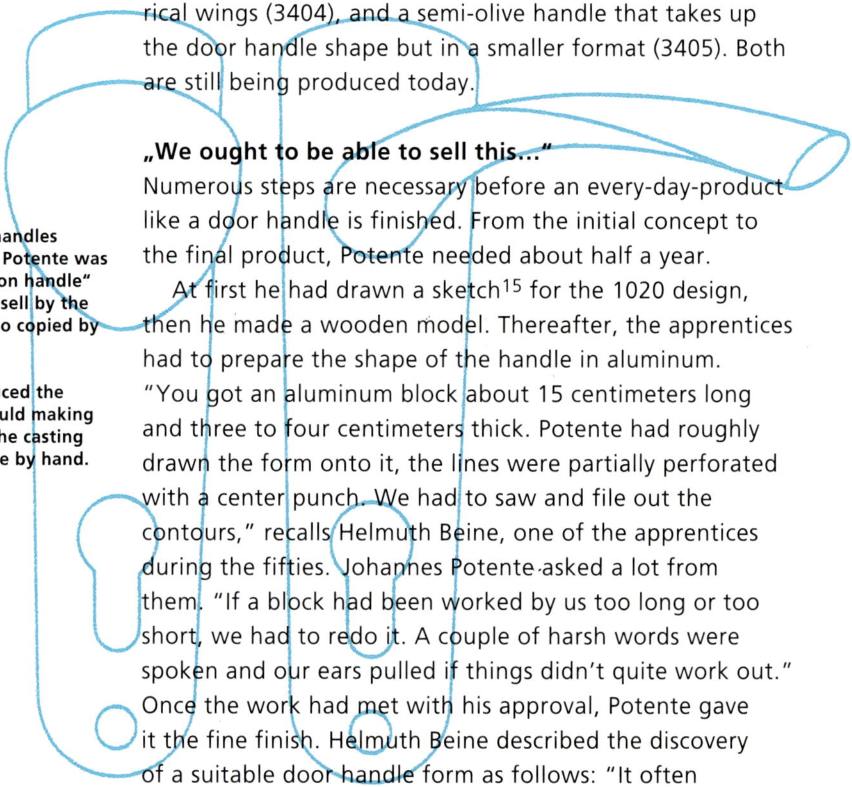

One of the first door handles designed by Johannes Potente was model 1034, the "million handle" (1952). Not only did it sell by the millions, but it was also copied by the millions.

In 1958/59 FSB introduced the copying jig for the mould making process. Before that, the casting moulds had to be made by hand.

would walk through the enterprise, pulling the model out of the pocket of his work coat to have the other employees test it: "Just grab the handle. Does it feel good in your hand? Do you like it?" [16]

In the case of molded-to-the-hand fixtures, as is the model 1020, both a right and left part were required for a pair because they have an actual upper side and can't be used on both sides of the door. As a result, two models, a right and a left, had to be built with the assistance of templates. Afterwards, the new door handle model 1020, the so-called primal model, was given to the managers of the enterprise for "tasting". At FSB, new models aren't checked but tasted, like a good meal. Potente is said to have presented the handle to Fritz Scheffler, the "taster-in-chief", with the words: "we ought to be able to sell this".

When the decision was finally made and the door handle was to be produced, they commenced with the manufacturing of the mold, the gray cast iron form. This was not an easy procedure. At first, the original model was traced onto a template. This meant that metal sheet templates that would delineate all dimensions had to be created. Following these templates, the gray cast iron molds were hand-chiseled in several parts. This was before the existence of copy milling by which the model could be traced using a machine. You had to consider carefully: "where do you separate the handle. Which side is placed into the top and which into the bottom half. That alone is pretty complicated. If you have a simple form, the separation level is flat and in the center. If you have a more complicated form, the separation level is more complicated, too", explains

The making of a door handle. The liquid aluminum is cast into the mould. It is placed in a so-called mould clamp in order to be opened and closed at the casting table.

Removed from the first cast and roughly planed, the new door handles are moved into the fine detailing workshop.

Dieter Eller.[17] And the form of the door handle 1020 was very tricky. Therefore, it wasn't and is still not very easy to produce. The only thing that was geometrically and technically corrected was the so-called guide shaft (where the handle neck is), a channel that was worked into the mold. A square shaft was inserted into this channel to provide the space for the square pin in the handle neck. This was the only component that could be accomplished by a machine; everything else was manual labor.

Next, the contours of the handle were copied onto the gray cast iron block with templates and, if possible, roughly planed on a planer. The other contours were manually worked out of the mold with a hammer and chisel. The form had to be constantly counter-checked against the templates. Then the cast form was riffled and cleaned up. The mold for model 1020 consisted of three parts. Today, however, only two parts are required because of technological advances. With a hand depth indicator that Johannes Potente had manually produced, he was able to measure the depth of the molds for the right and left handle in order to determine whether they were identical. Only after everything was fine were the first test castings carried out. Given its asymmetrical form, there is still a lot of manual labor involved in the production of the model, and production robots generally cannot be used or can only be used to a very limited extent.

New technology – new forms: aluminum casting

After World War II aluminum casting was increasingly utilized. Aluminum is a very malleable material; it can be

welded, pressed, pulled, embossed, forged, rolled out into foil and cast into almost any form. Aluminum is the most important light metal as well as the most available one. Its melting point is at approximately 700 degrees Celsius. Due to the high energy cost for the first winning, it is an expensive material; however, it can be recycled repeatedly. And for the recycling, only a fraction of the energy necessary for the first winning is required.

In 1951/52, FSB established a contemporary light metal foundry. Aluminum casting had been known earlier, but its use was not very widespread in the fixture industry. This new technology opened up many unexplored possibilities. Now there was much more freedom in the design, and suddenly forms were being created that hadn't been possible with the traditional technologies such as forging, embossing from sheet metal or the metal working technology (deep-drawing). Now, light metal molds were being used.

Door handles in tinted aluminum: no. 1051 and 1020 by Potente, 1057 by Jan Roth, 1034 by Potente (from front to back).

Pure aluminum is covered by a dense, hard and water-resistant layer of oxidation. Thus, the metal becomes highly resistant to corrosion and against many corrosive substances such as alcohol, acetic acid, glycerin or aqueous acids. This protective layer can also be created and strengthened artificially: after the aluminum handle is finished mechanically, it is anodized. In an electrochemical process, the surface is converted into aluminum oxide. This oxidization, or anodized layer, can be stained thus offering additional design possibilities.

Currently, the 1020 handles are stained in the following colors: new silver, brass, bronze, dark bronze. Additionally, there is the natural silver. After the staining process, the surface is again treated in order to obtain even more resistance to corrosion. Today, as during Potente's time, the model 1020 is produced in aluminum, but it's also available in brass.

When the first handles of the 1020 line were cast in 1954, the new model was presented at the Cologne Hardware Fair. Among others, the two owners of the company, Fritz Scheffler and Maximilian Schneider, the sales manager (domestic), the order manager, the works manager, the authorized signatory, and the sales representatives – about five at the time – were present. Each one of them carried a new door handle model in their pocket and tried to appraise it. The specialized dealers were approached with words like "listen, you can sell this, can't you? How many are you going to take"? [18] Back then, they kept line lists to keep track of how many handles were sold per day. The dealer cost for the model was DM 8,50. The sales price was determined by those behind the counters back then and not, as is the case today, by the purchasers who base their decisions on economic factors rather than on whether or not they like the form.

After the fine work on the door handles – here model 1020 – is done, they are placed into a galvanizing bath. Here they are covered with a protective layer that can also be tinted.

Up to 1997, about three million copies of the door handle 1020 had been sold, approximately 50,000 per year on average. The handle received a big following especially during the sixties and seventies and about twice as many were sold per year, i.e., about 100,000 during this period.

The organic molded-to-the-hand fixture

Johannes Potente's door handle 1020 has its foundation in

the tradition of the organically designed molded-to-the-hand fixtures. They are oriented towards the hand and their form is adapted to the hand. This is why they feel more comfortable than the more edgy forms.

The first new door handle of the post-war era appears to have been an organically shaped door handle by the Graeff Brothers from Wuppertal-Elberfeld. It had soft, rounded forms that included the handle neck and was thicker towards the end of the handle.

In 1951, Wehag in Heiligenhaus, the traditional enterprise that FSB – still a young company in the fixture industry – looked up to with awe, published 14 new door handle models. Eight of them were designed by the Berlin architect Max Schuhmacher; in the catalog, they were all described as "hand form fixtures". They were "...models characterized by a distinct handiness and individual forms. They are, as the name says, completely adapted to the grasping hand". [19] Schumacher had already designed two molded-to-the-hand fixtures for Wehag in 1939 (no. 90 and 91). One of the two handles, model number 90, similar to Potente's 1020, has a soft organic curve which, however, doesn't form a wave. An earlier molded-to-the-hand fixture with an organically curved handle is the model no. 23 by Wilhelm Riphahn which he designed for Wehag in 1931. The handles by Schuhmacher and Riphahn were the first molded-to-the-hand fixtures whose designs were determined by the form of the hand. Both display characteristics of the streamline form.

The term "hand form" dates back to the thirties and refers to edgy Art Deco door handles. But we're not referring to those here. Schuhmacher's door handles from

Even after he had retired, Johannes Potente couldn't let go of the door handles – shown here while filing a model in his workshop.

1951 are developments of anatomical, molded-to-the-hand fixtures[20] that were combined with elements from the kidney-shaped table culture. Often, the pivoting point (thumb stop) is kidney-shaped. The long cover plates are also asymmetrically curved. The Wehag model no. 86 by Schuhmacher is also marked by a curve that starts at the pivot point but is much flatter than in the FSB model 1020.

Potente definitely knew the common door handles of his time. He was in close contact with the sales representatives and thus learned what was in demand and also had them obtain models from the competition. From around 1950, he regularly went to the Cologne Hardware Fair where he had the chance to study the competition's products and get the catalogs from other fixture enterprises.

The organic direction in molded-to-the-hand fixtures was represented up to the mid-fifties above all by Wilhelm Braun-Feldweg. Like a sculptor, he shaped his early handles, including the handle necks, with hollows and indentations in his work for Erno (Ernst Nofen Bronzewarenfabrik). In an advertisement by the enterprise, they say about the handles by Braun-Feldweg: "handle forms are derived from the process of gripping, the way the human hand wants to grasp... today the architect, especially, looks for simple organically developed forms... If on one hand he looks for a decent profile, he knows on the other hand to appreciate the better and handier form of this profile... Their common characteristic is that they both offer themselves to the grasp of the hand."[21]

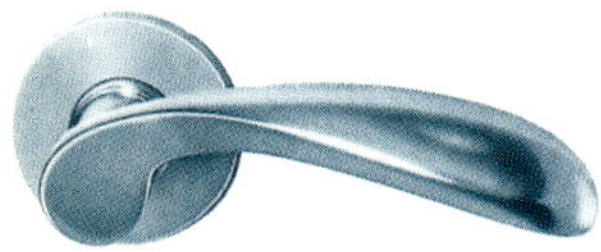

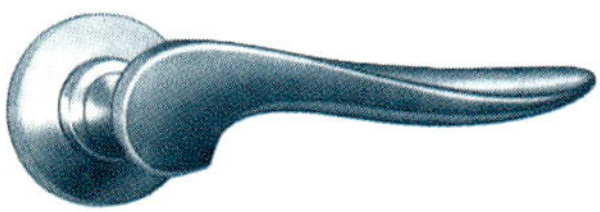

The Berlin architect Max Schuhmacher designed the molded-to-the-hand-fitting No. 90 for Wehag in 1939.

In 1931, the door handle No. 23 by Wilhelm Riphahn had already been designed. Together with Max Schuhmacher's handles, it belongs to the first molded-to-the-hand-fittings that are designed according to the ergonomics of the hand.

Like Johannes Potente, Wilhelm Braun-Feldweg was a craftsman and had apprenticed as a steel engraver. The door handle no. 127 that he designed in 1952 (almost simultaneous to Potente's 1020) drives the organic hand form to its peak. Like in the case of Potente's handle, a wave form runs through it which is, however, less curved and declines towards the end. Potente's handle is by far less adapted to the hand than Braun-Feldweg's no. 127. The latter almost seems to have been organically grown – Braun-Feldweg didn't design the model on a piece of paper but pressed his own hand into a roll of plasticine. [22] He worked this hand imprint, a negative of his own hand, into a door handle. One disadvantage of such organically designed molded-to-the-hand fixtures is that they are too adapted to specific palm sizes and in most cases predetermine a certain grasp position.

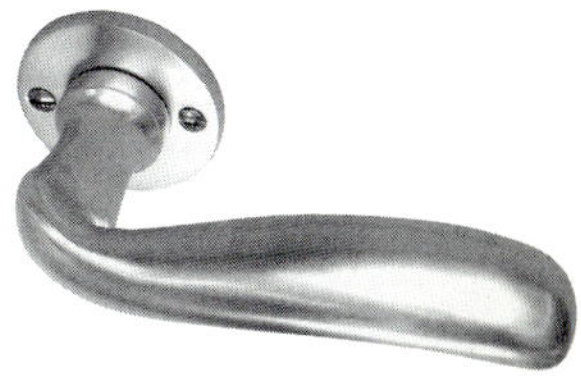

Wilhelm Braun-Feldweg carried the organic molded-to-the-hand-form to an extreme in 1952 with the door handle No. 127 that he designed for Erno. The basis was his own hand print.

Another handle with a wave-shape comes from Italy. It was designed by Sergio Asti and Sergio Favre during the first half of the fifties. Here, contrary to Potente's handle, the curve is dynamic and strong. The handle, with its pits and grooves, is designed in a very sculptural fashion. Reminiscent of a bone, the end of the handle, which declines at an angle, looks somewhat like the back of a spoon. The handle neck is conical and narrows but grows thicker towards the pivoting point. Yet another Italian door handle, named *Velasca* by BBPR (an architectural office founded in Milan in 1932, Gianluigi Banfi, Lodovico Belgiojoso, Enrico Peressutti and Ernesto Nathan Rogers) and designed in 1956 for Olivari in Borgomanero, belongs to the family of organically curved handles. Here, the

Das tapfere Schneiderlein.

FSB

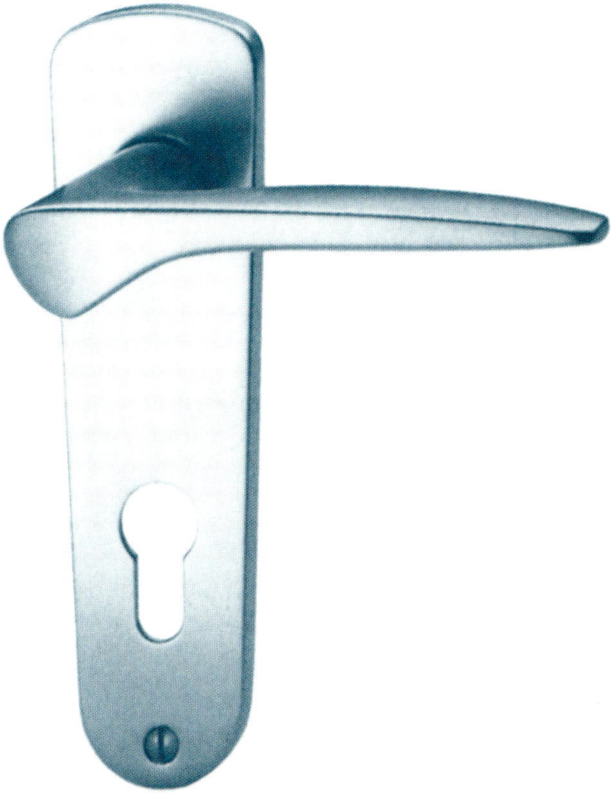

curved line starting at the round pivot point seems to end in a relatively straight handle surface.

The curved door handle models keep reappearing. The *Vaippa* handle by the Finnish designer Timo Sarpaneva (1963) has a curve that runs in an arch from the top to the bottom and thus doesn't change its direction as does Potente's 1020. In 1997, the Danish designer Erik Magnussen designed the model no. 1128 for FSB. At first, he had designed model no. 1127, which imitates the wing-beat of a sea-gull. Following the idea of his wife, Jonna, who wanted a more feminine design, he developed a "smaller wing-beat". This door handle is characterized by a soft curve that unquestionably reminds one of Johannes Potente's no. 1020 and is called "hand charmer" by the enterprise.

Preceding double-page: from the mid-fifties onward, Potente moved away from the organically curved to the factually geometric door handle designs. This development can be clearly seen in model 1051, the so-called "Schneider handle". Left: dashing in his uniform – Franz Schneider Jr., the son of FSB's founder.

Curved door handles reminiscent of model 1020 emerged time and again – for example, no. 1127 designed for FSB in 1997 by Erik Magnussen.

Potente's door handle 1020 may be a molded-to-the-hand fixture with soft organic forms, but it wasn't worked in a sculptural way as the organically molded handles by Braun-Feldweg were. It's neither as playful nor as exaggerated in its design as are some of the other molded-to-the-hand fixtures from the first half of the fifties. It's precisely this clarity and simplicity that make it a classic that has been produced and sold since 1954. Potente's door handle evokes associations with the kidney-shaped table culture; it doesn't deny the fashion of the times, but it is timeless enough to have survived up to the present, contrary to other organically formed molded-to-the-hand fixtures from the fifties.

From Johannes Potente's only preserved text we are able to learn how he imagined a well-designed door handle.

He wrote it in 1957 at the occasion of a legal copyright trial that was to challenge the copying of the door handles 1020 and 1034, and the long cover plate 7507: "The function of a door handle is very clear. As far as the form is concerned, it is given a very high value, especially today, for the simplest door constructions of modern door design. The door fixture, especially the door handles with the matching long cover plates or rosettes, are to provide the door with a special accent. More than ever, the consumer demands – and he is taught to do so – proper function, functional realization, appealing appearance and good design from the most simple of everyday objects. And quite often the design is the primary factor for the choice and decision for a purchase. A traditional form or line originating in past style perceptions is not what is desired, but instead, a contemporary, factual and useful one." [23]

Around the mid-fifties, Johannes Potente's door handle designs became much clearer, more factual and geometric; he turned away from the organic forms. During this time, he designed the balanced and elegant model 1051, which became a synonym for the entire enterprise as the "Schneider handle". The bestseller was most likely realized in 1958. The thumb stop has the shape of a triangle rounded on one side and merging with the narrow, straight-lined, tapering handle. The handle has a distinct index finger hollow and the other two "laws of grasping" – ball support and grasping volume – are also present. This door handle was copied by many, but none of the copies ever reached the balanced harmony of the original.

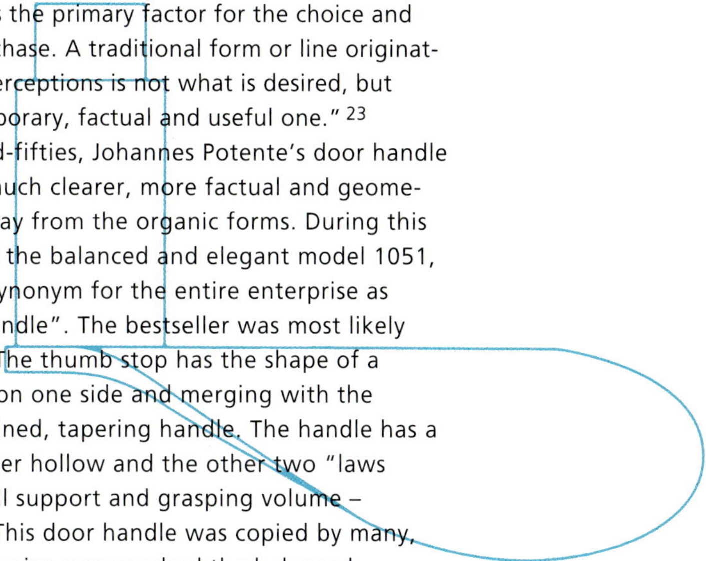

Der Brakel-Schnabel.

FSB

Simultaneous to the "Schneider handle", the so-called "beak handle", model no. 1024, was created. It got its nickname from the long, pointed triangle on the front side that is suggestive of a duck's beak. Viewed from the top, the handle surface is wide and tapers towards the pivoting point.

About two years later, Johannes Potente redesigned the form of the "Schneider handle" (1051). The result was the lean, clear model 1058 which became Potente's favorite model from that point onward. The triangular accent at the pivoting point had been abandoned. What was left was a narrow surface that softly tapers towards the back. Viewed from above, the handle has the same form as model 1051.

Preceding double-page: the clear geometric "beak handle" (no. 1046) got its nickname due to the long, stretched-out triangle reminiscent of a duck's beak.

Potente's door handle 1020 was often copied or served as a model – obviously for this model with a hammered surface structure.

From anonymous form maker to top designer

Johannes Potente is no longer anonymous. In the meantime, several of his door handles – among them the model 1020 – have even been requested by the Museum of Modern Art (MoMA) in New York for the evaluation and acceptance procedure. Paradoxically, Otl Aicher contributed decisively to this fact. And yet, during his lifetime Potente designed his door handles without self-promotion and outside the glaring lights of publicity. And according to Aicher, this was perhaps a great advantage: "maybe he wouldn't have done a few things if he had presumed: humanity, at least from a cultural perspective, is watching me. Thus, he was able to preserve his uncontrolled casualness. It is precisely that personal quality which is a component of his eagerness and documents his unrelenting occupation with the subject itself and not with its effect. His dialog with door handles would perhaps have ceased if he had suddenly found himself no longer alone, but with the design critic and historian looking over his shoulder." [24]

To Otl Aicher, it's the craftsman who establishes human culture. "An anonymous designer doesn't care about his style. He has none. He is, like a craftsman, alone in his workshop. He's interested in the result. Human culture is based on this attitude." [25] And he continues: "if someone works for an enterprise, they work differently than a designer who wants to see his work exhibited in the Museum of Modern Art in New York." [26]

Only eight years after his name had first appeared in public, Johannes Potente advanced in the press from an anonymous form maker to a top designer whose name was being mentioned in the same breath as the stars of the industry. In a 1996 article on today's in-house designer at FSB, Hartmut Weise, we can read: "Today, his name [Hartmut Weise] can be found next to top designers like Johannes Potente, Dieter Rams, Jasper Morrison or Philippe Starck..." [27]

Following double-page: advertising campaign from 1993/94: the model 1020, at times called "wing beat," next to the opened doors of the classy fifties' car that look like the wings of a hovering bird.

Notes

1 *Neue Westfälische* no. 291, 12/15/1988; conversation of the author with Jürgen W. Braun, manager of FSB in Brakel, on 2/16/1998.

2 Otl Aicher: "die unterschrift. kunst und design", in: Otl Aicher, Jürgen Werner Braun, Siegfried Gronert, Robert Kuhn, Dieter Rams and Rudolf Schönwandt: *Johannes Potente, Brakel. Design der 50er Jahre*, Cologne 1989, p. 78.

3 Ibid. p. 78.

4 Conversation of the author with Dieter Eller, Potente's nephew and the current head of product development with FSB on 2/16/98 in Brakel.

5 Semester report of the Badische Kunstgewerbeschule in Pforzheim.

6 Jürgen W. Braun: "Das Leben des Johannes Potente", in: *Johannes Potente, Brakel*, loc. cit., p. 47.

7 Anniversary publication: *Ein Blick durchs Schlüsselloch. 75 Jahre FSB*, Brakel 1957.

8 Dieter Eller believes that Potente gave up school for financial reasons because he had to earn his living on the side.

9 Conversation of the author with Helmuth Beine and Dieter Eller on 2/16/98 in Brakel.

10 Otl Aicher, loc. cit., p. 78.

11 Siegfried Gronert: *Türdrücker der Moderne. Eine Designgeschichte*, Cologne 1991, p. 44.

12 Bernd Meurer and Hartmut Vincon: *Industrielle Ästhetik: Zur Geschichte und Theorie der Gestaltung.* Werkbund-archives, vol. 9, Giessen 1983, p. 619.

13 Conversation of the author with Dieter Eller, loc. cit.

14 Conversation with Johannes Zimmermann and Heinz Schäfers on 2/17/98 in Brakel. According to their recollection, first the interior door handle, then the house door handle and finally the light handle was designed. In 1955, all three versions were already being offered.

15 Proper construction drawings were made with FSB only from 1958/59 upon the purchase of copying mills. In Johannes Potente's office, a small drawing office with drawing boards was installed back then.

16 Conversation of the author with Helmuth Beine on 2/16/98 in Brakel

17 Dieter Eller, loc.cit.

18 Helmuth Beine, loc. cit.

19 Citation from Gronert, loc. cit., p. 46, Wehag catalog 1951, p. 18.

20 Gronert, loc. cit., p. 46.

21 In: *Bauen und Wohnen*, 1954, p. 44.

22 Wilhelm Braun-Feldweg: *Normen und Formen industrieller Produktion*, Ravensburg 1954, pp. 149 and Gronert, loc. cit. pp. 48, 57.

23 Johannes Potente, unpublished manuscript from 11/11/1957, FSB archives

24 Otl Aicher, loc. cit., p. 78.

25 Ibid.

26 Ibid.

27 Rolf Antrecht: "Comeback der Spinner", in: *Capital*, issue 10, 1 October 1996, pp. 79.

Bibliography

Aicher,Otl/Braun, Jürgen Werner/Gronert, Siegfried/Kuhn, Robert/Rams,Dieter and Schönwandt, Rudolf: *Johannes Potente, Brakel. Design der 50er Jahre*, Cologne 1989
Braun-Feldweg, Wilhelm: *Normen und Formen industrieller Produktion*, Ravensburg 1954
Cascini, Stefano: *L'architettura presa per mano. La maniglia moderna e la produzione Olivari*, Milan 1992
Gronert, Siegfried: *Türdrücker der Moderne. Eine Designgeschichte*, Cologne 1991

Photo Credits

All images courtesy of FSB, Brakel

Franz Schneider
Brakel GmbH + Co
Nieheimer Straße 38
D-33034 Brakel
Fon +49 (0) 52 72 608 - 0
Fax +49 (0) 52 72 60 83 - 00

76-36

Forever young.

FSB

Service
If you would like to receive our catalog, please contact us:

Verlag form.
Books & Magazines on design issues.

Telephone +49 (0) 69 94 33 25-0
Facsimile +49 (0) 69 94 33 25-25
e-Mail: form@form.de
http://WWW.form.de

Impressum

Translated into English by:
Katja Steiner and Bruce Almberg

Editor:
Volker Fischer

Editorial Department:
Anne Hamilton

Graphic Design:
Sarah Dorkenwald,
Absatz, Gesellschaft für Kommunikations-Design,
Frankfurt am Main

Lithography:
Hans Altenkirch
Mediaproduktionen GmbH,
Nieder-Olm

Print:
Franz Spiegel Buch GmbH, Ulm

Die Deutsche Bibliothek –
CIP-Einheitsaufnahme
The door handle 1020 by Johannes Potente / Andrea Scholtz. [Transl. into Engl. by: Katja Steiner and Bruce Almberg. Ed.: Volker Fischer]. –
Frankfurt am Main : Verl. Form, 1998
(Design classics)
Dt. Ausg. u.d.T.: Die Türklinke 1020 von Johannes Potente
ISBN 3-931317-73-0